THE MOST BEAUTIFUL LANDSCAPES INCLUDE WILD HORSES

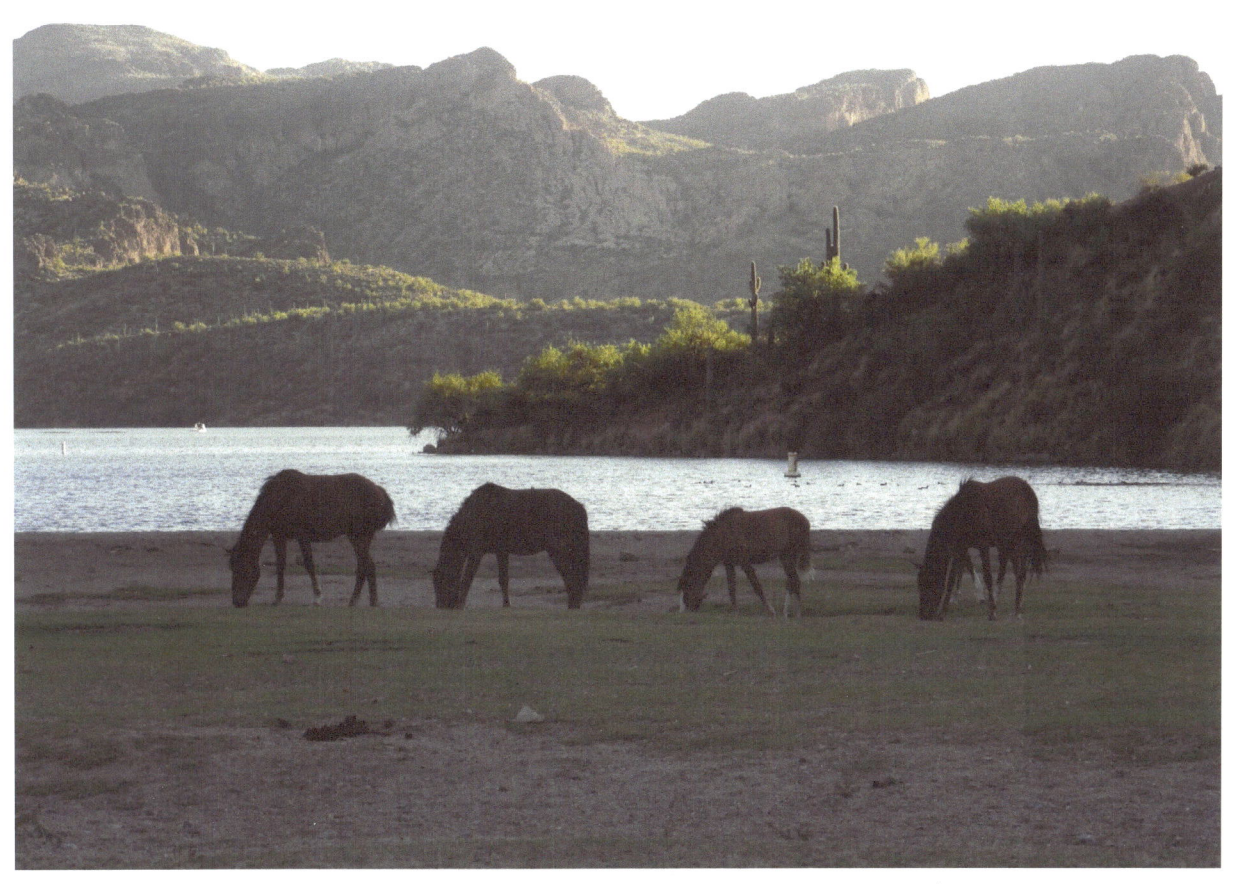

AS PHOTOGRAPHED BY
LARRY STIMELING

©2017 ALL RIGHTS RESERVED NAM-VET PUBLISHING;
Mesa, AZ 85216

PREFACE

Internationally known writer and poet Alice Walker Is quoted in my book Horse Sense as saying, "Horses make a landscape look beautiful."

That saying originates from a Native American wise man. He was referencing the beauty of the horses the white man brought to the Plains even as he was lamenting the migration of the white man's migration to the West.

In my short time in Arizona I have found the beauty of the desert. The majestic Saguaro, the beauty of mountains rising up in the midst of fields of desert foliage and the foliage itself are as magnificent as I have seen anywhere.

Yet in all its beauty the landscape is made even more beautiful by the wild horses. The images on these pages were all captured along the Lower Salt River near Phoenix, Az.

I hope these images give you a small sense of the beauty that one can only experience by actually being there.

The Most Beautiful Landscapes Include Wild Horses

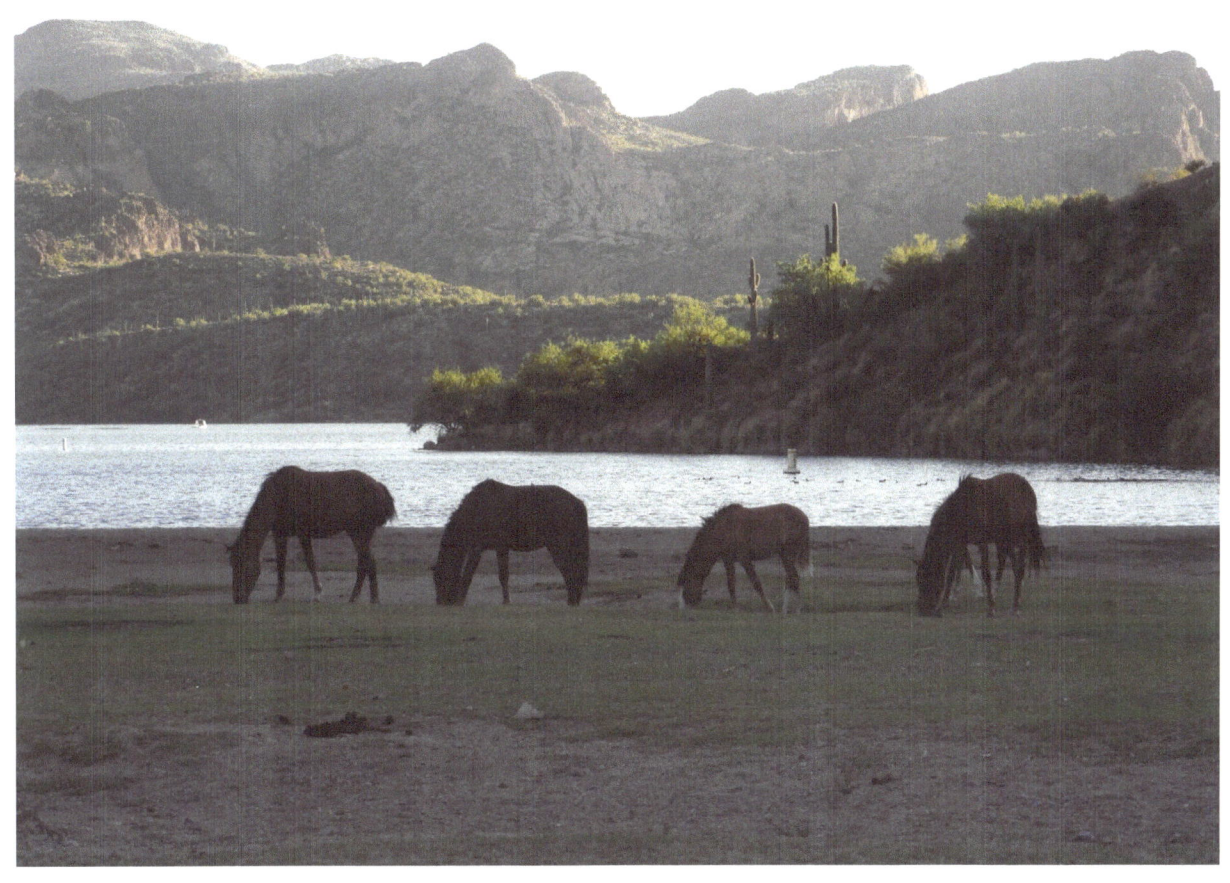

As Photographed By
Larry Stimeling

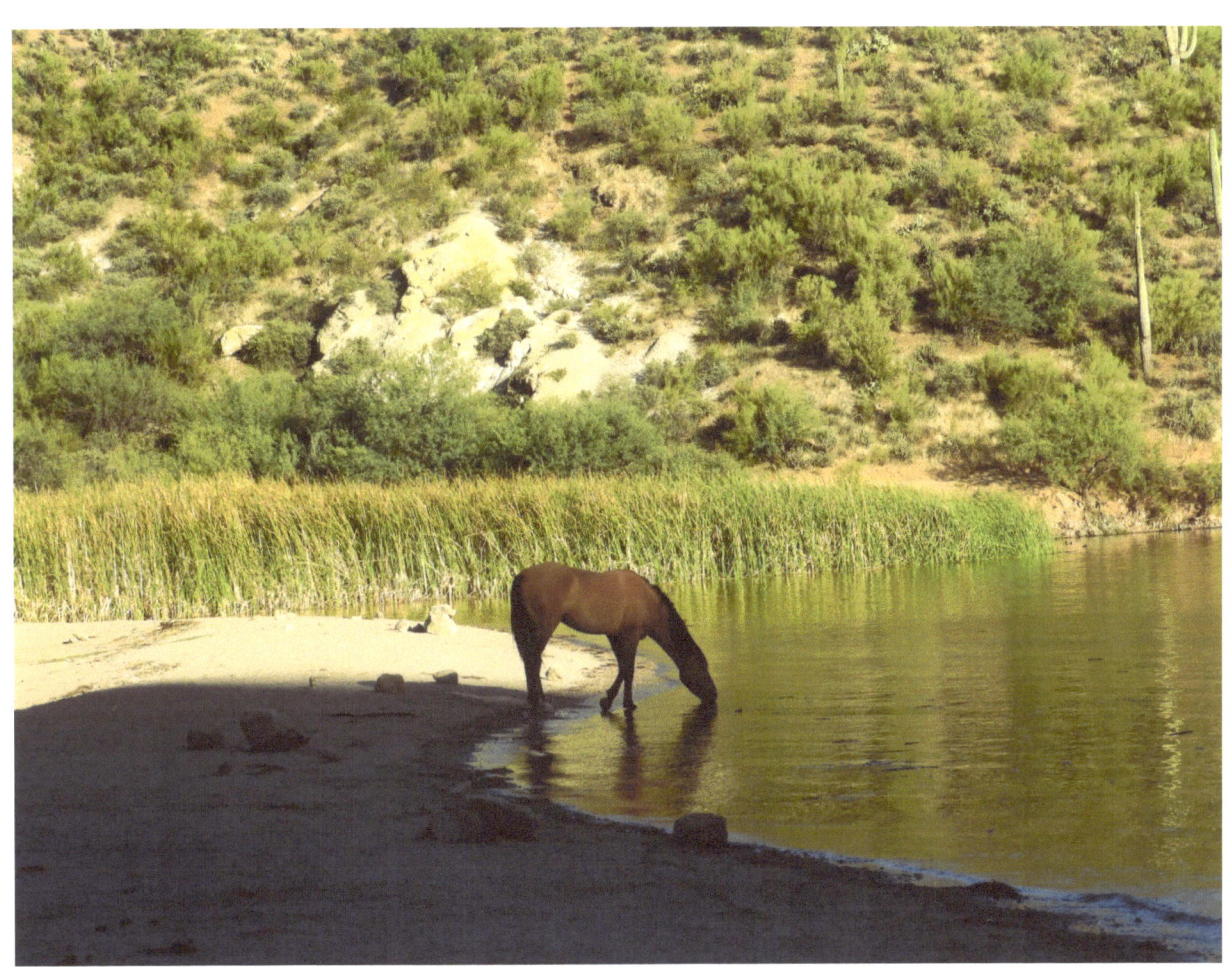

The landscape along the Lower Salt River includes views of tall grasses in front of rocky hills.

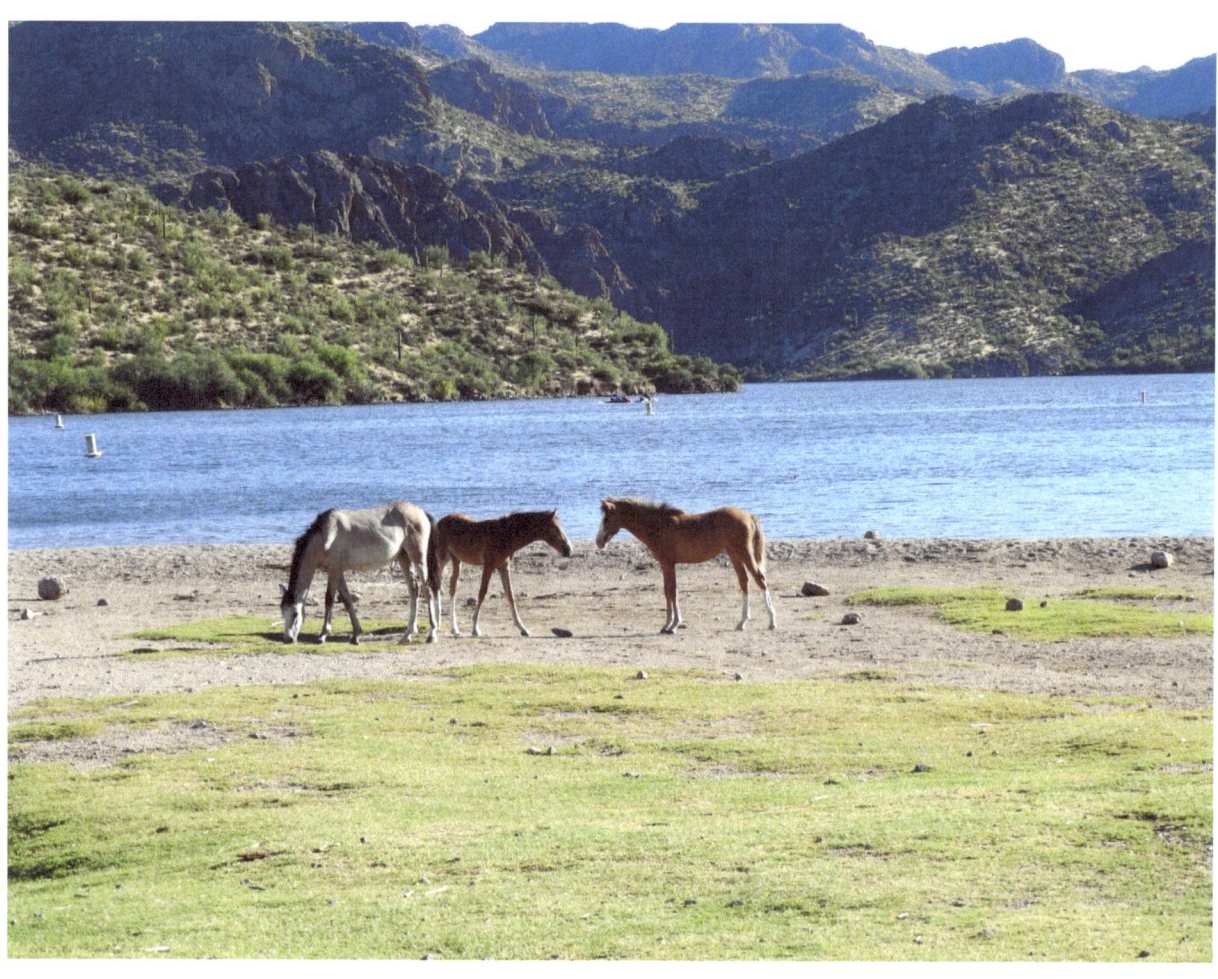

The water in the foreground highlights the mountains while both highlight the horses.

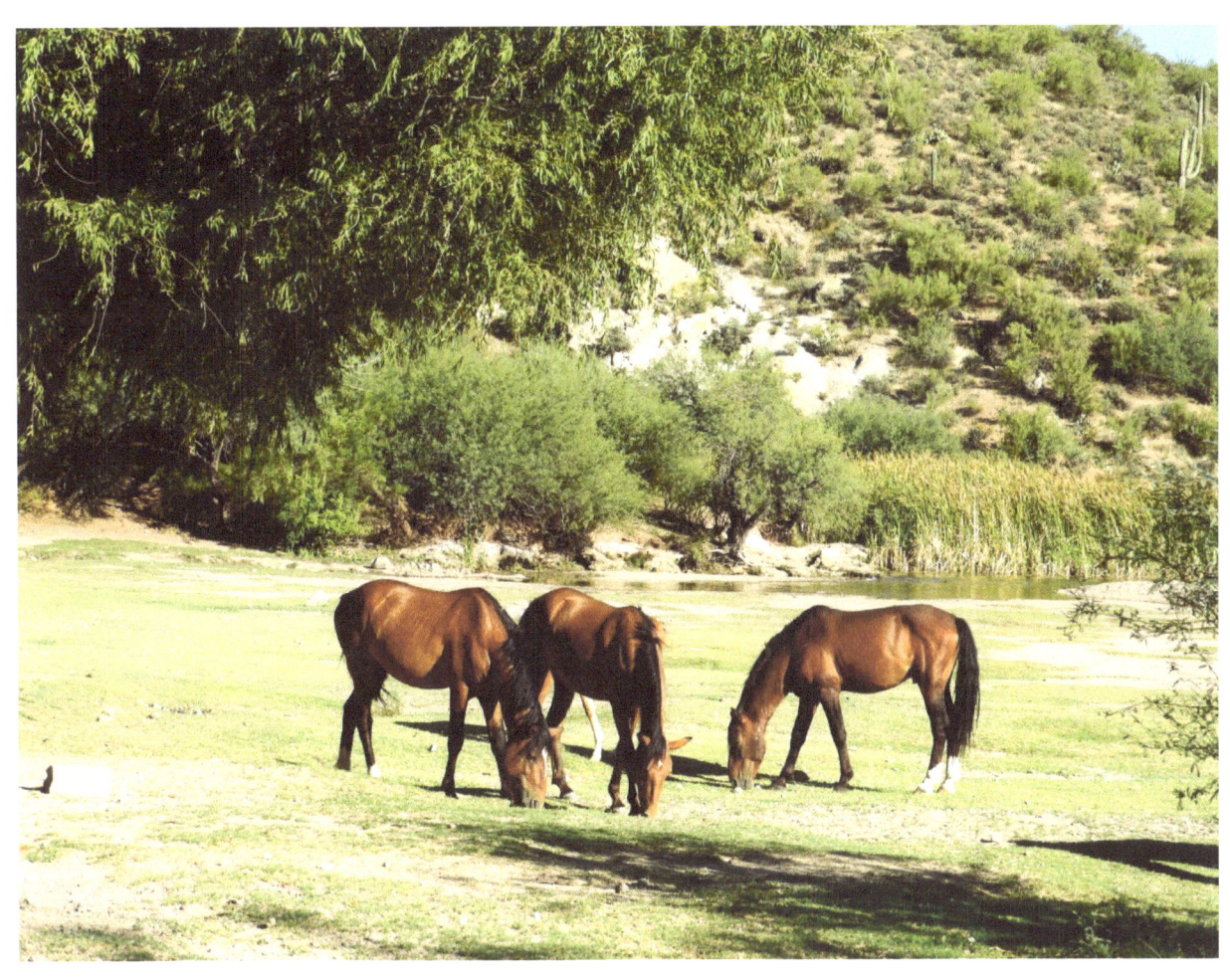

It matters not whether it is a few horses …

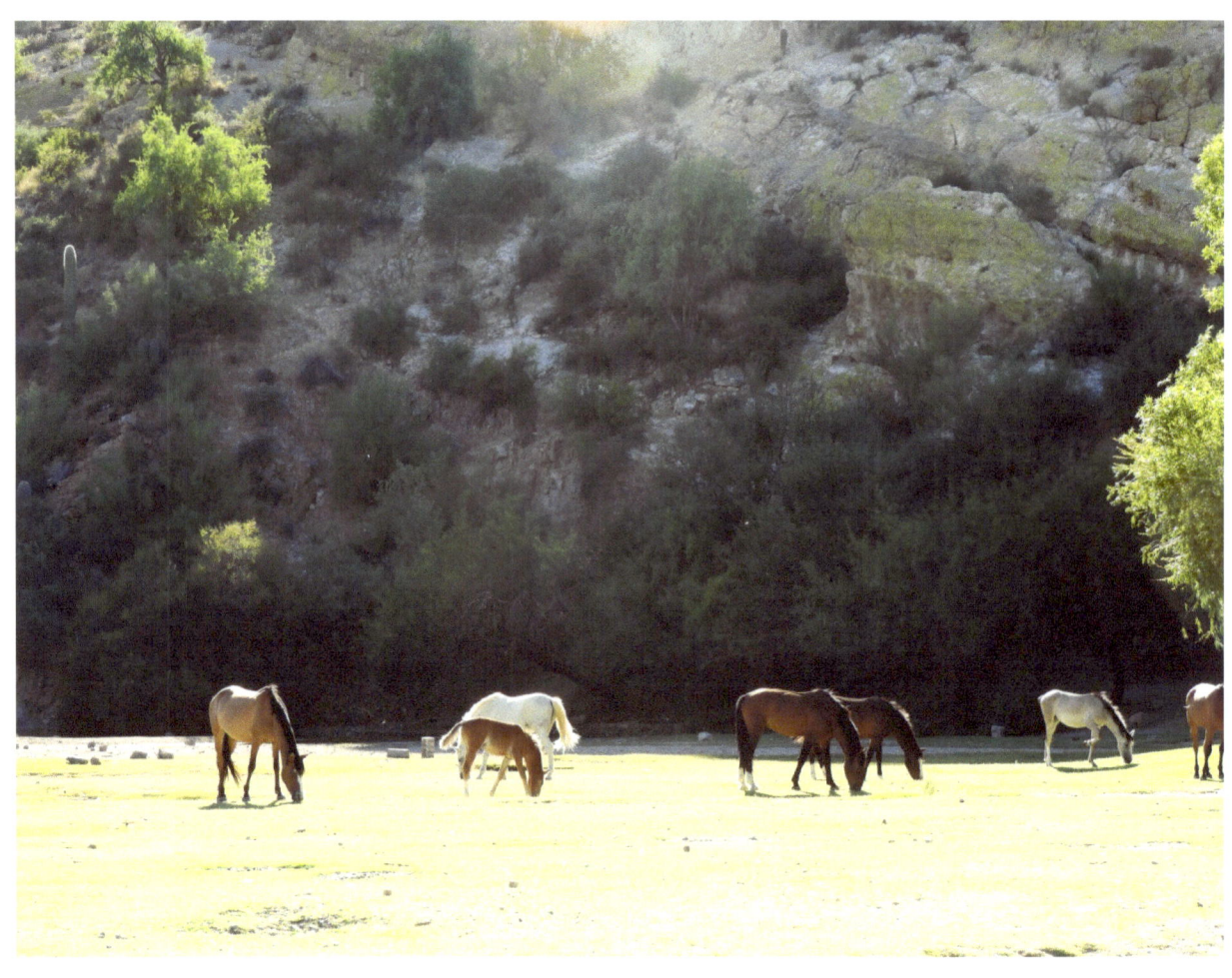

or an entire band …

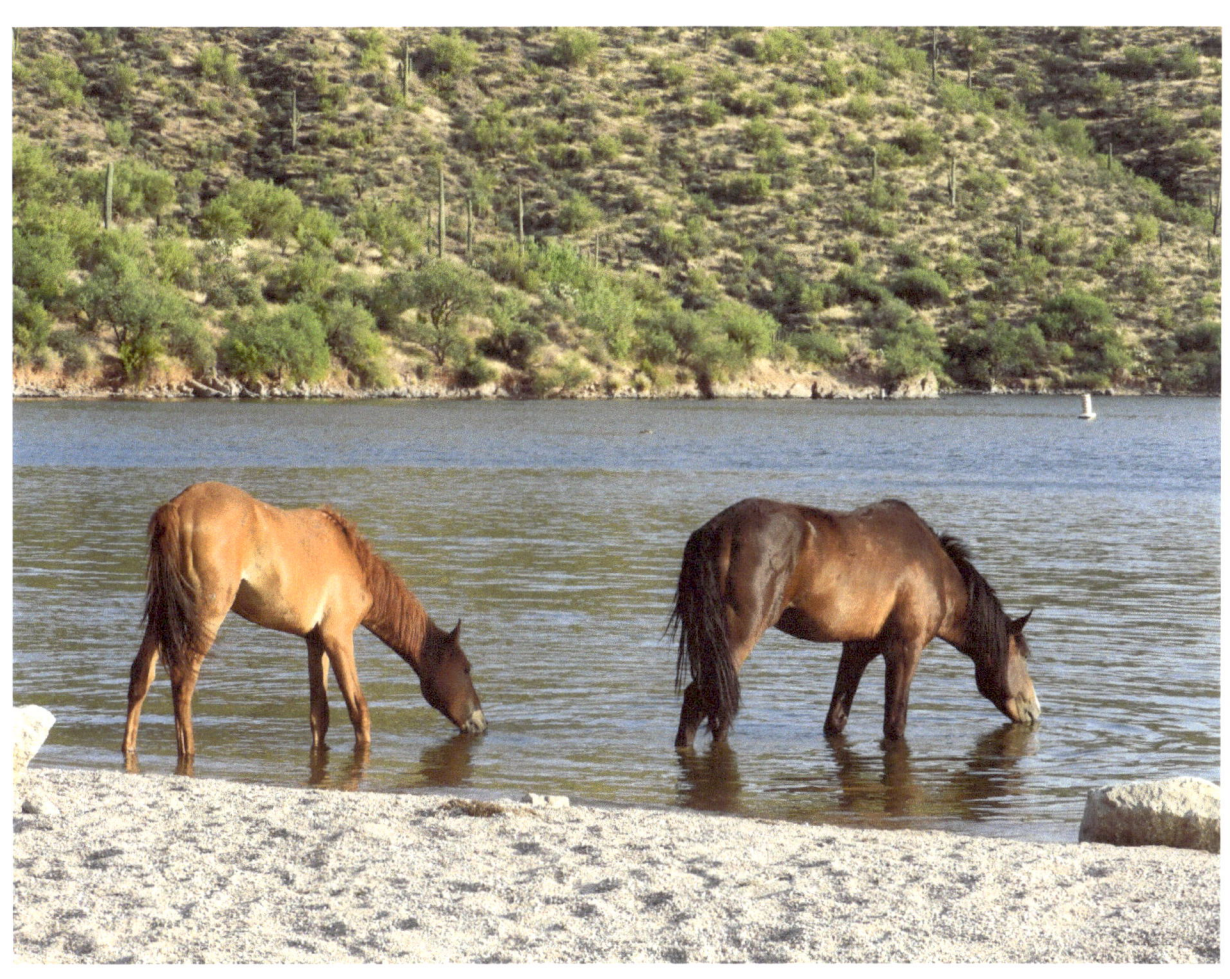

Even just a pair

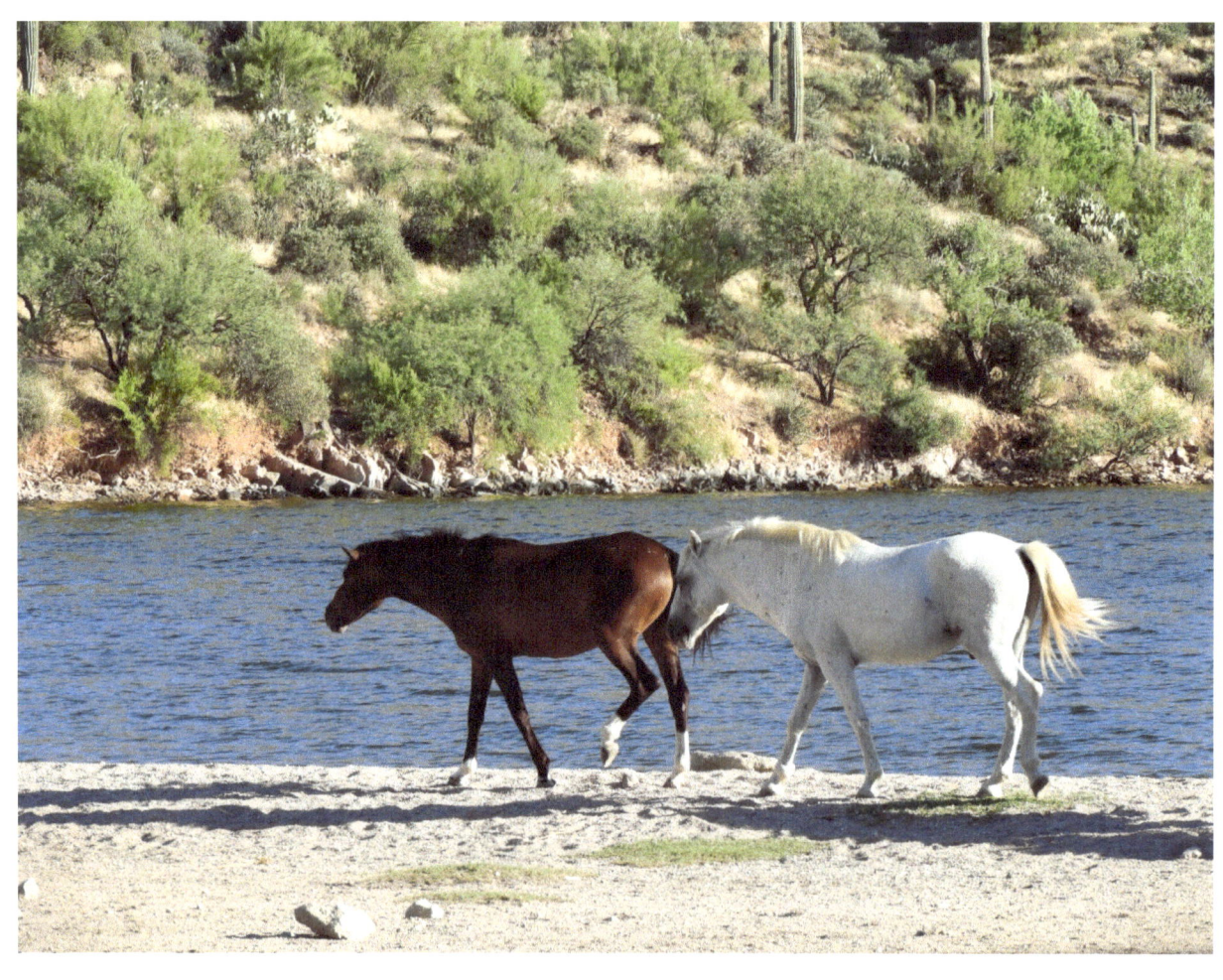

Wild horses adds to the beauty.

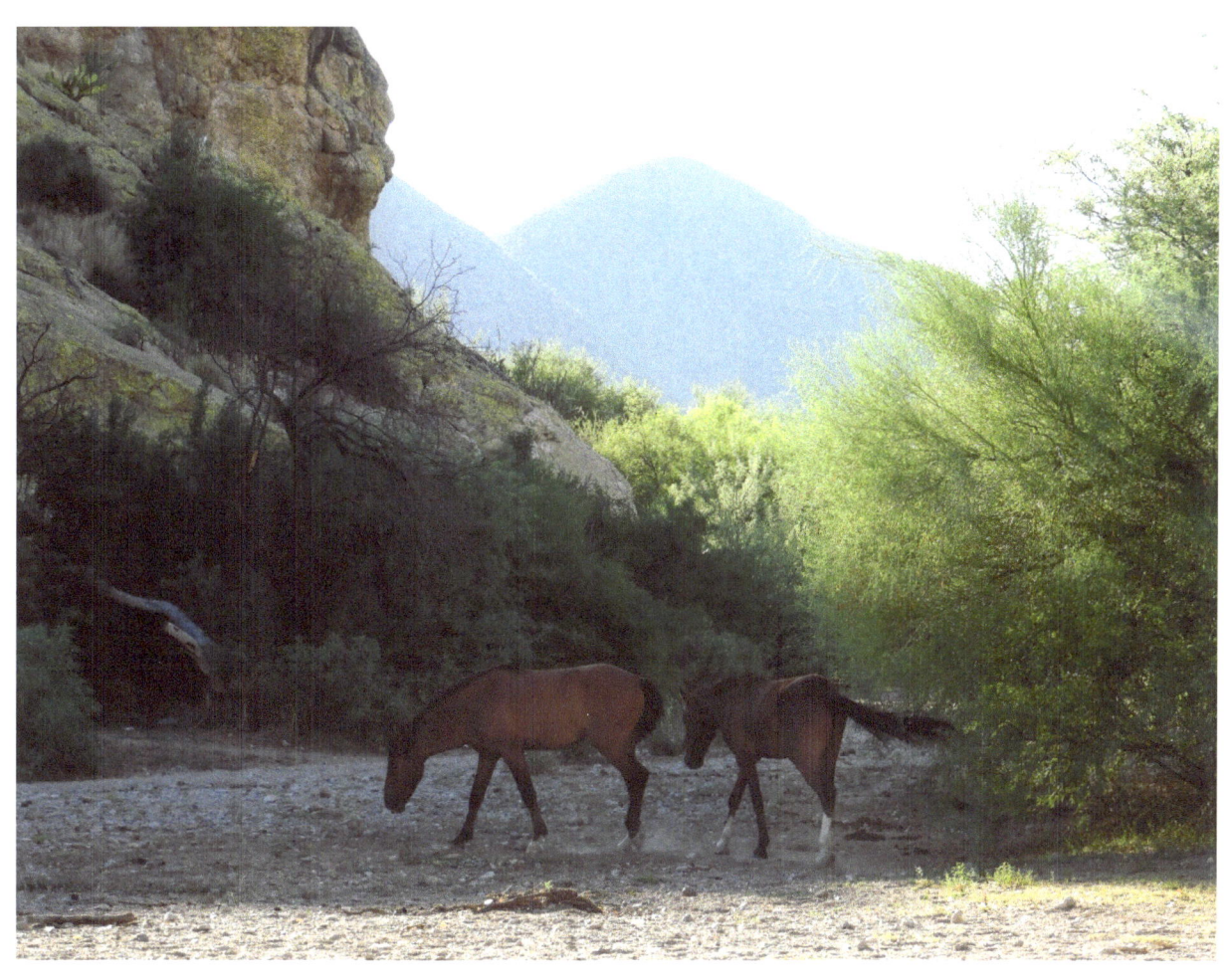

They have style.

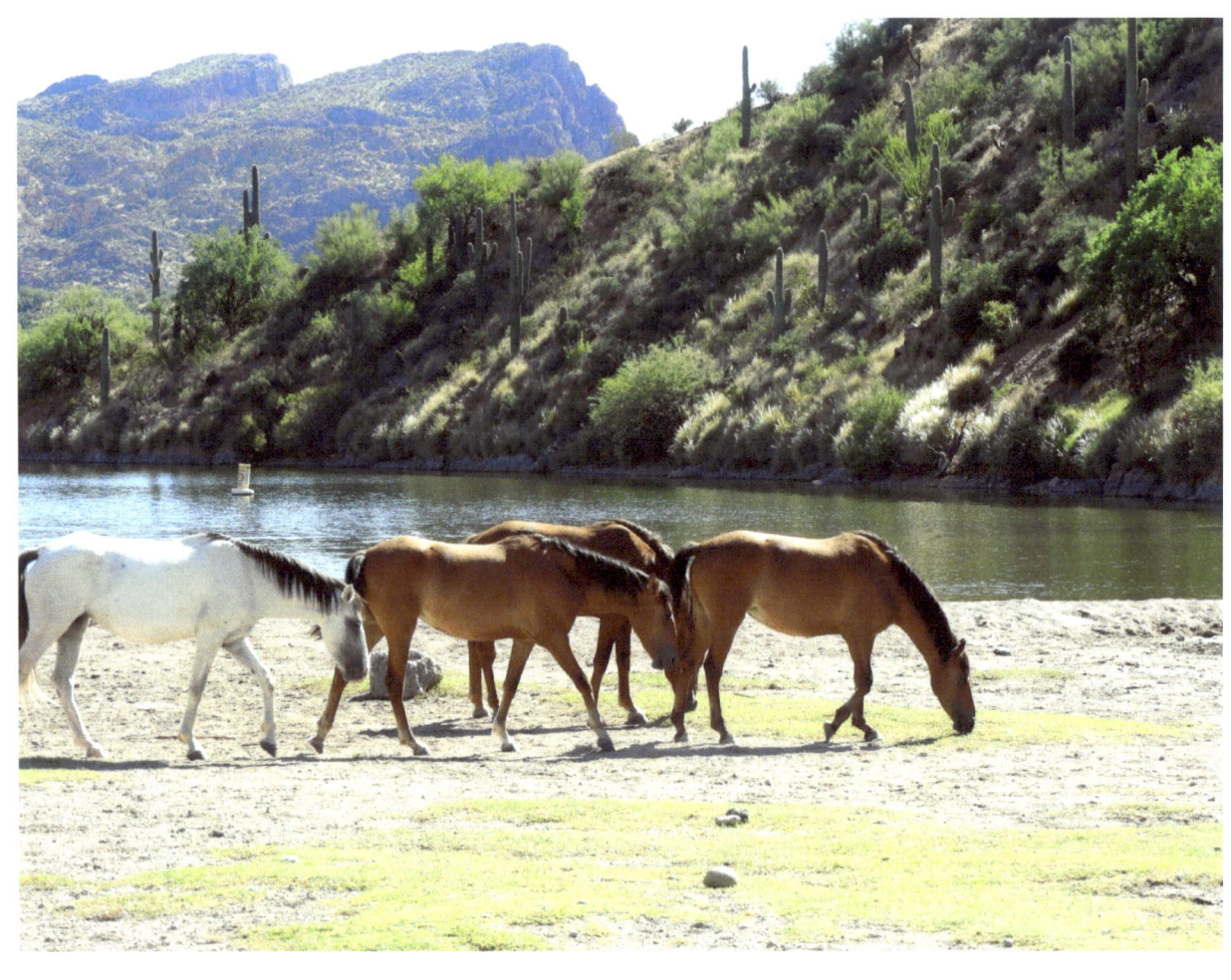

They have grace.

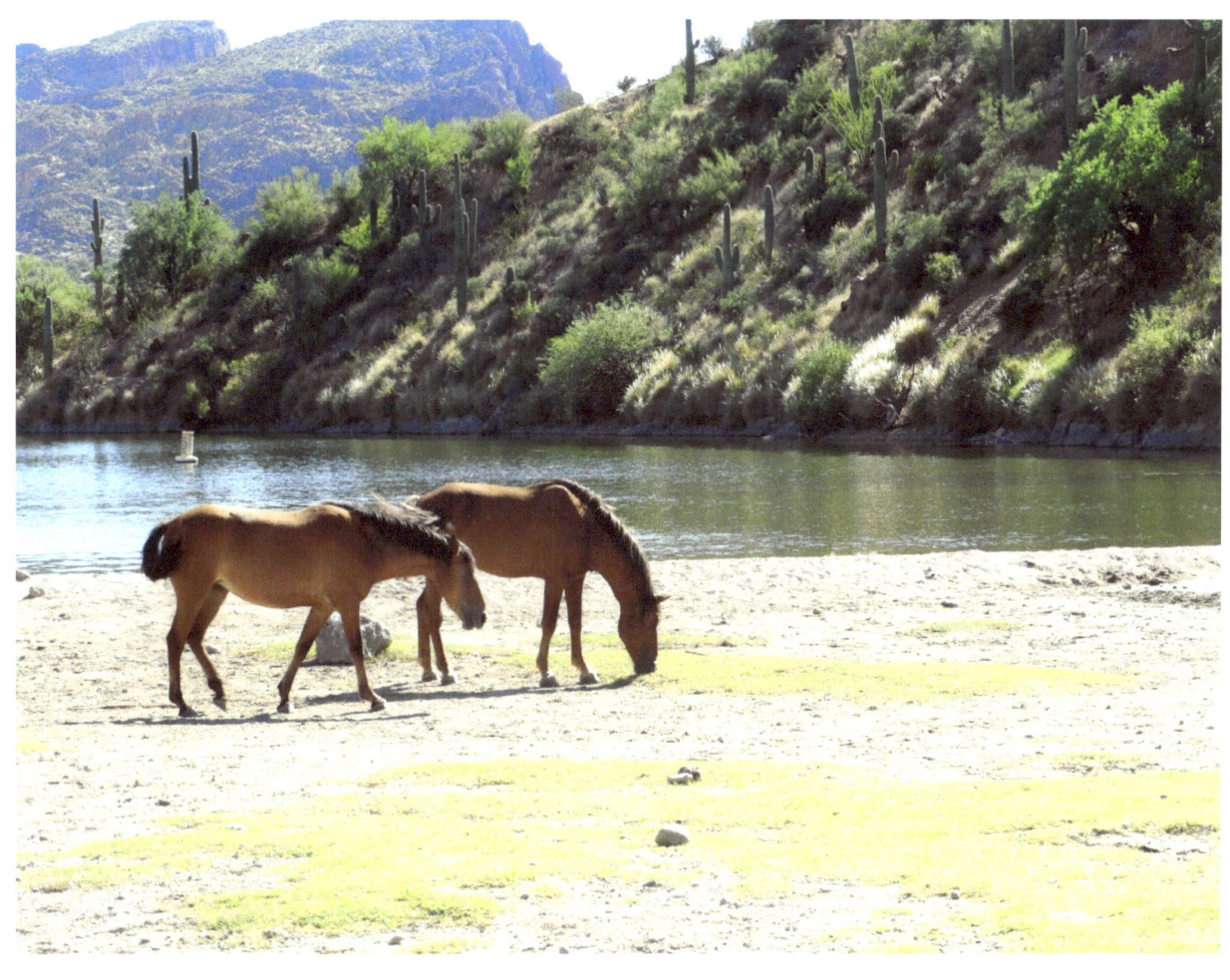

They're all winners.

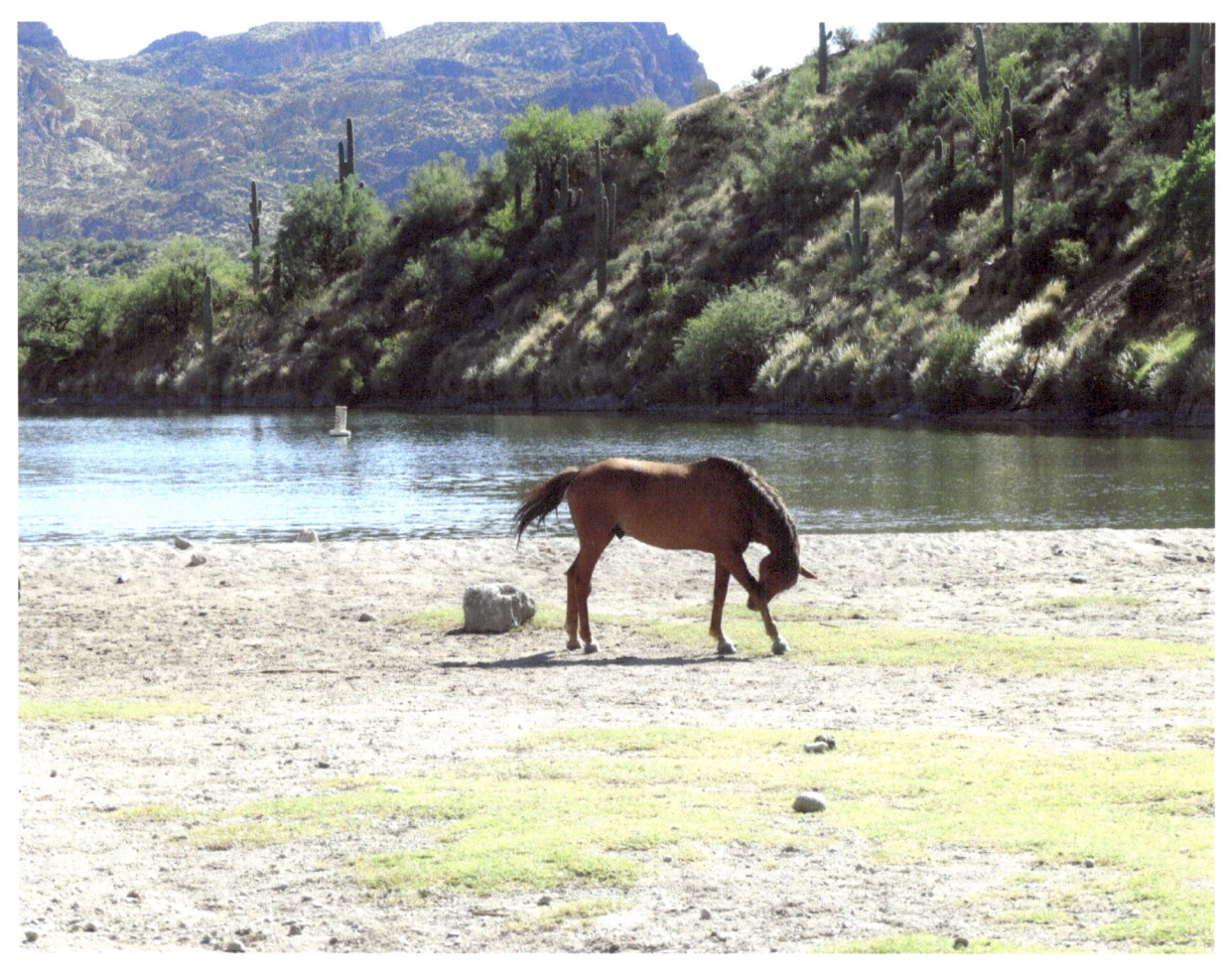

Actually, WE are the winners!

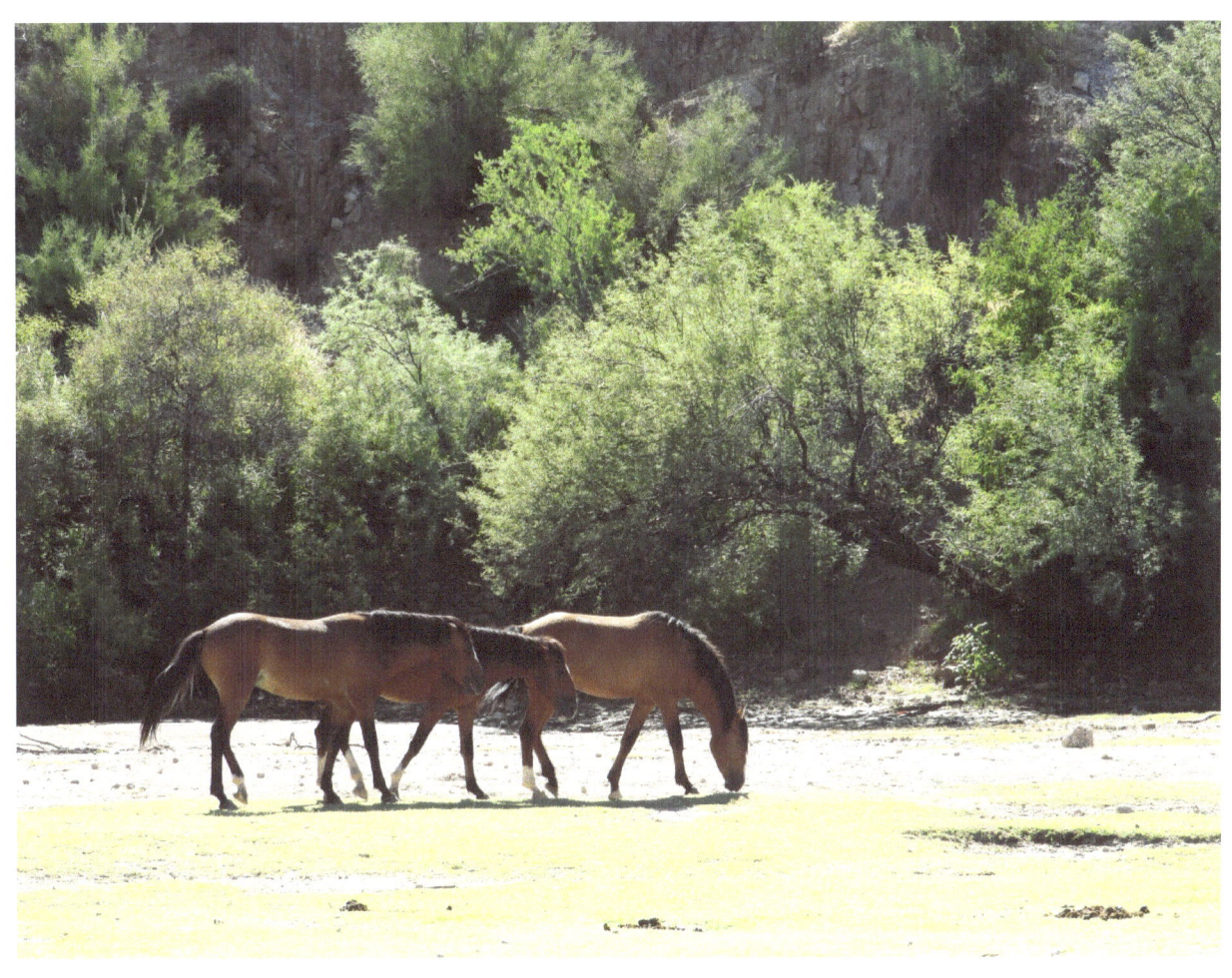

We have the eyes to enjoy the beauty of a landscape that includes wild horses.

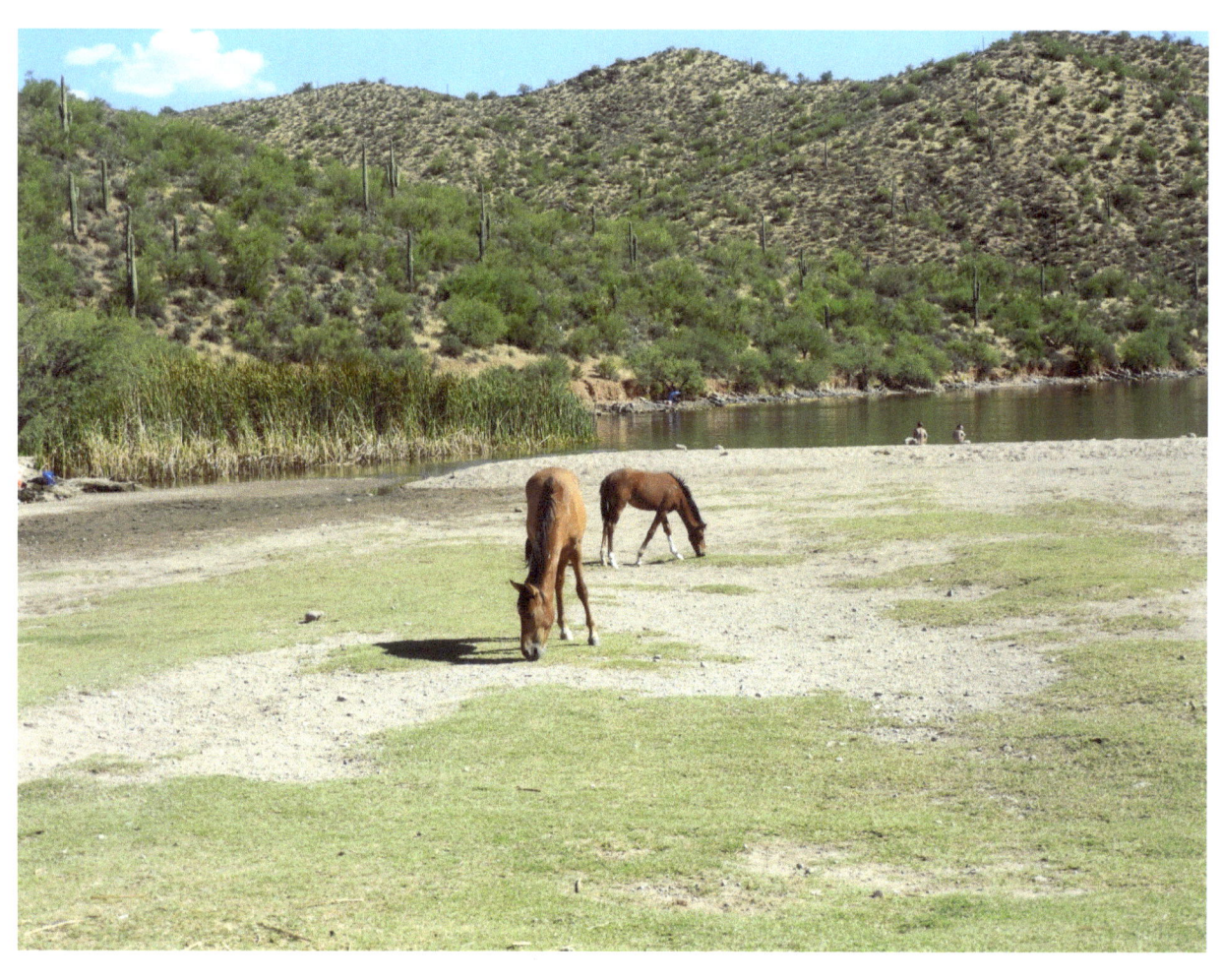

However this may not be the case for future generations.

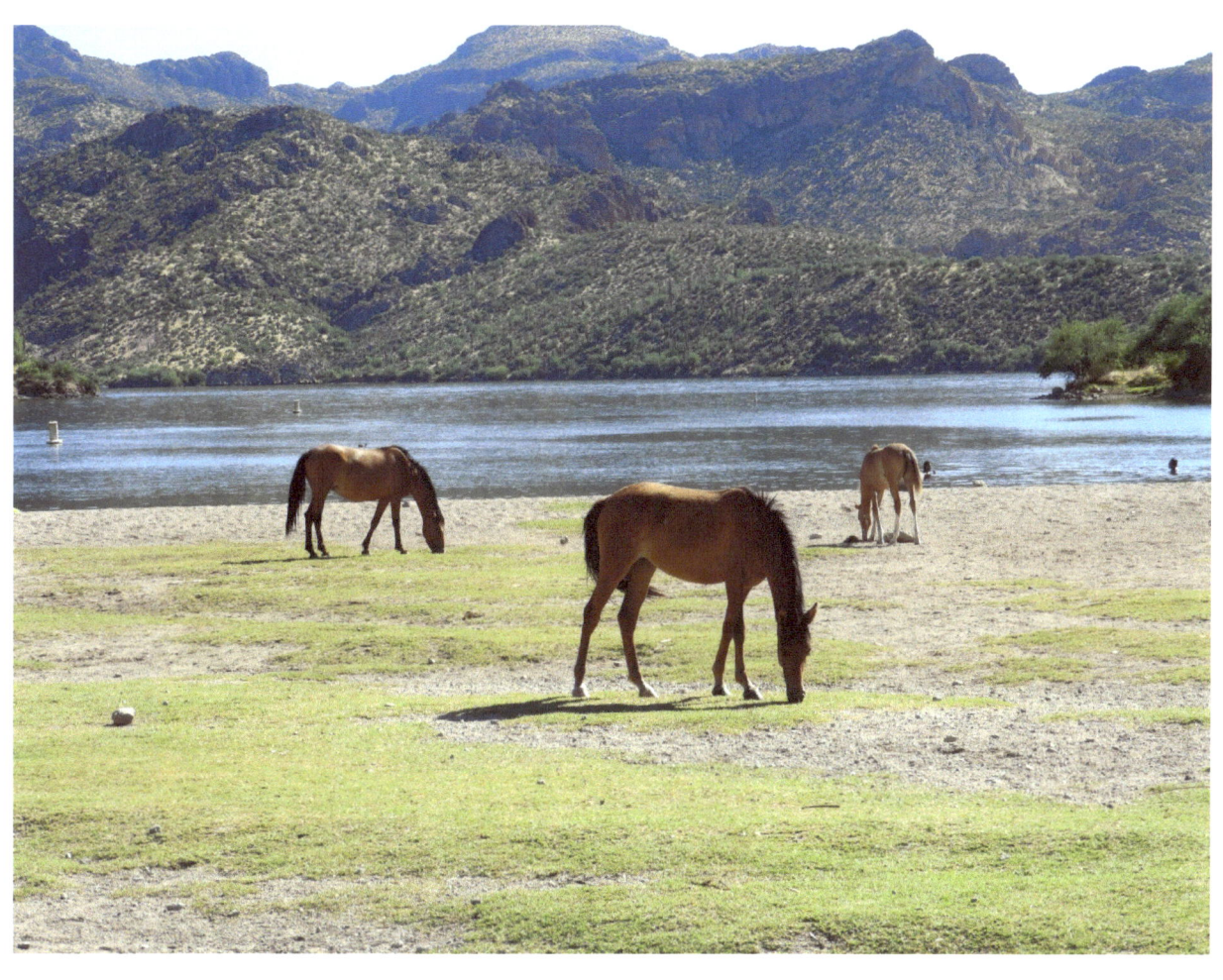

There is a battle brewing in the halls of Congress ….

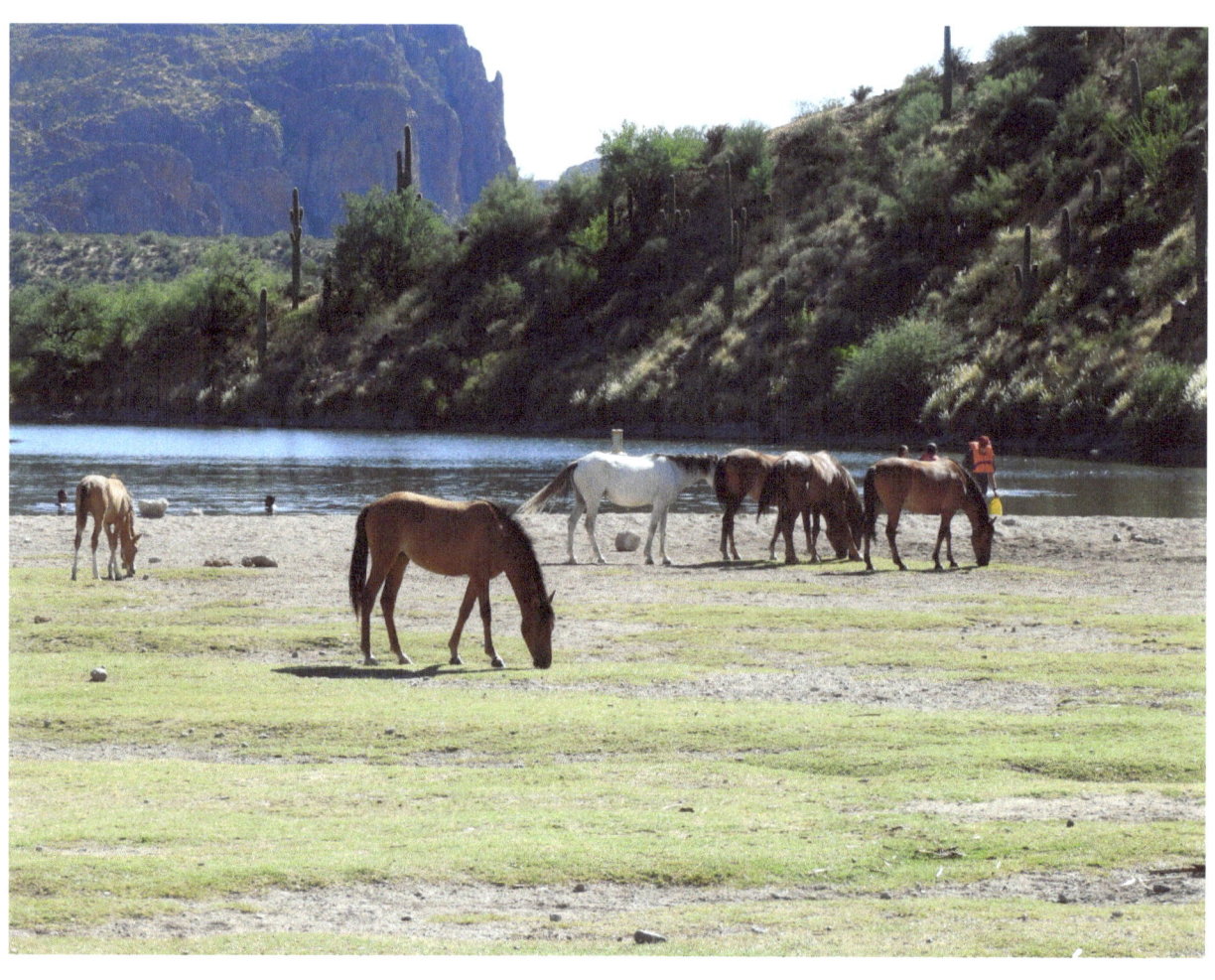

Pitting the wild horses against ranchers wanting use of more open range.

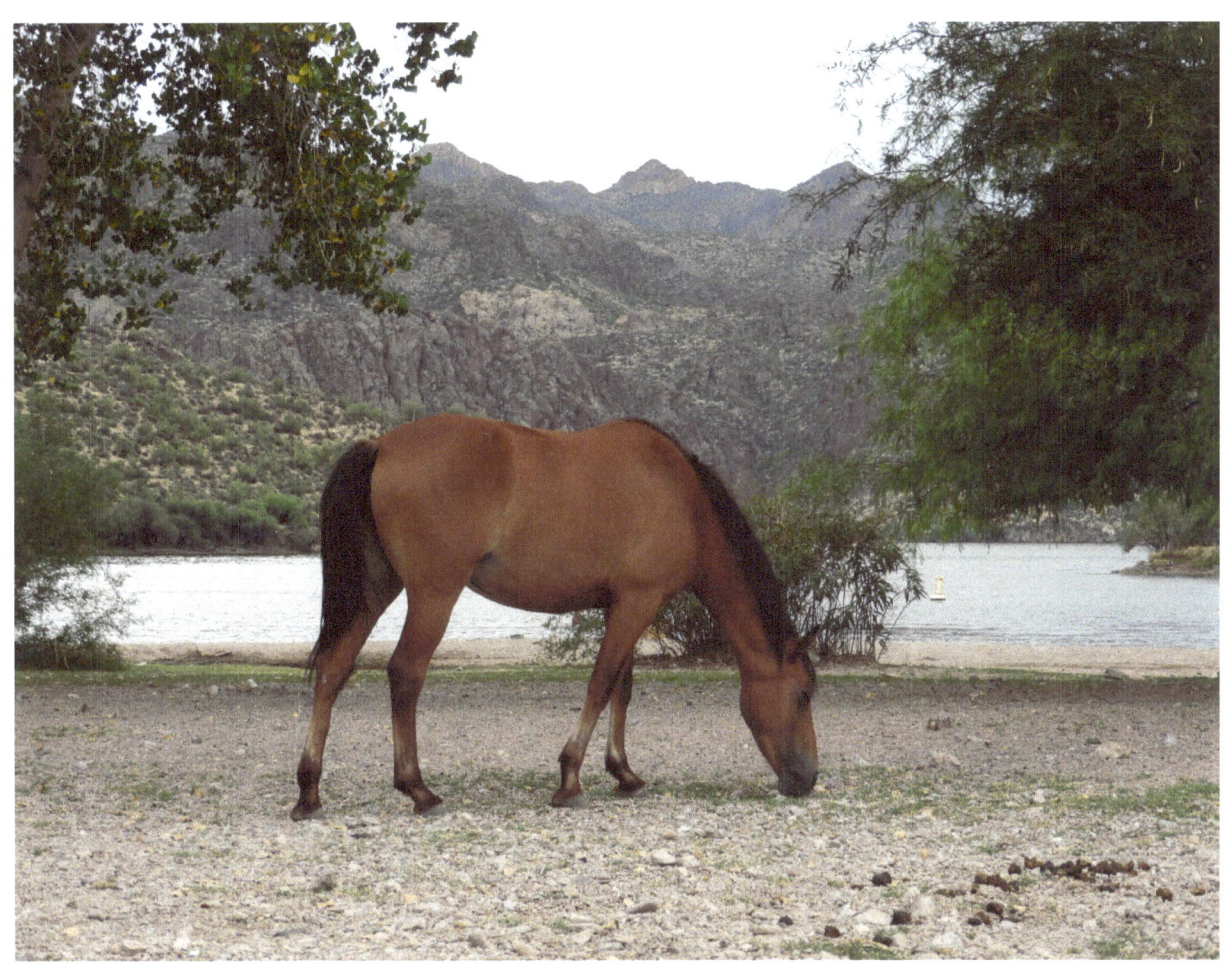

This puts the wild horses right in the middle.

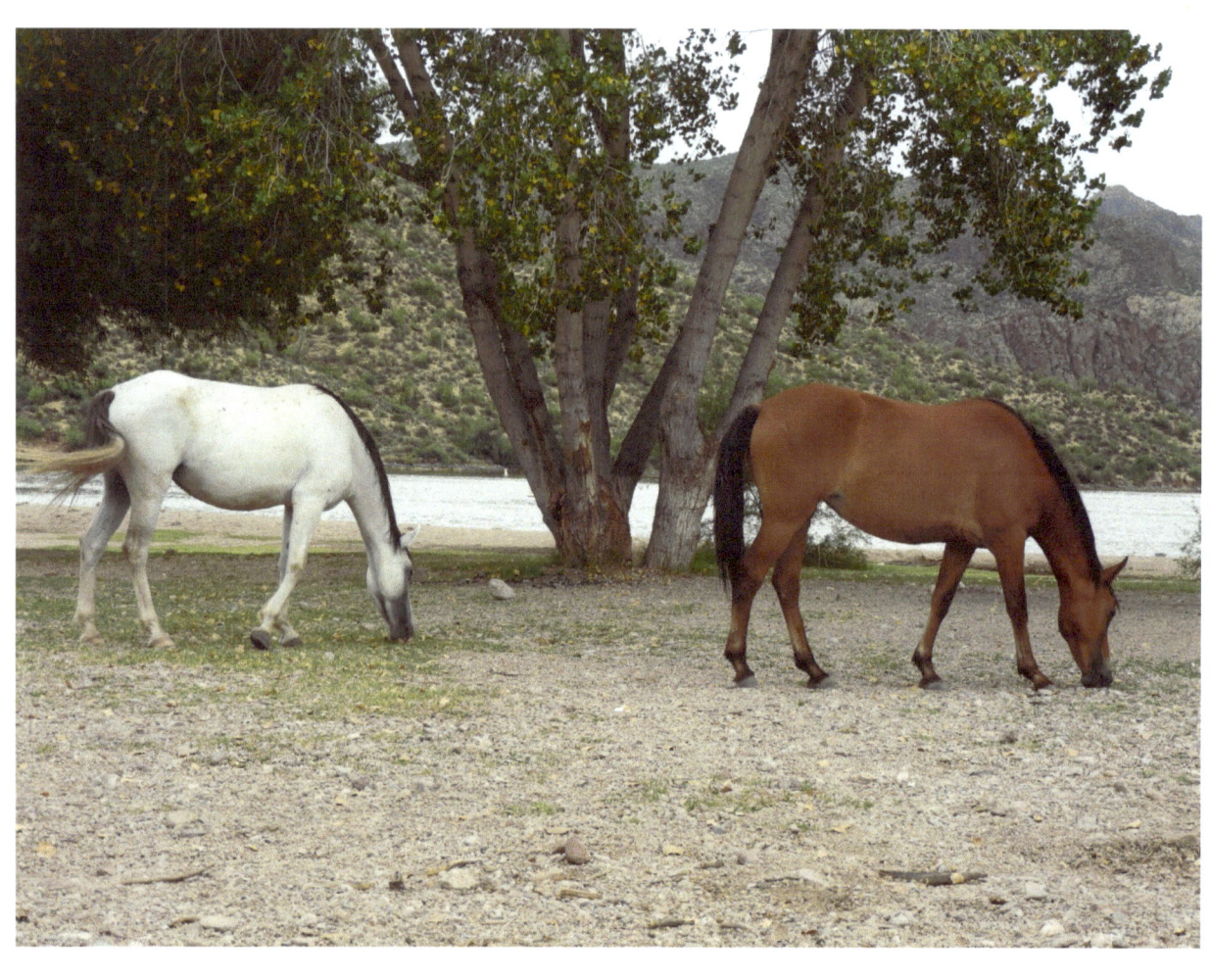

Almost 80% of Americans want to see wild horses on our Public lands

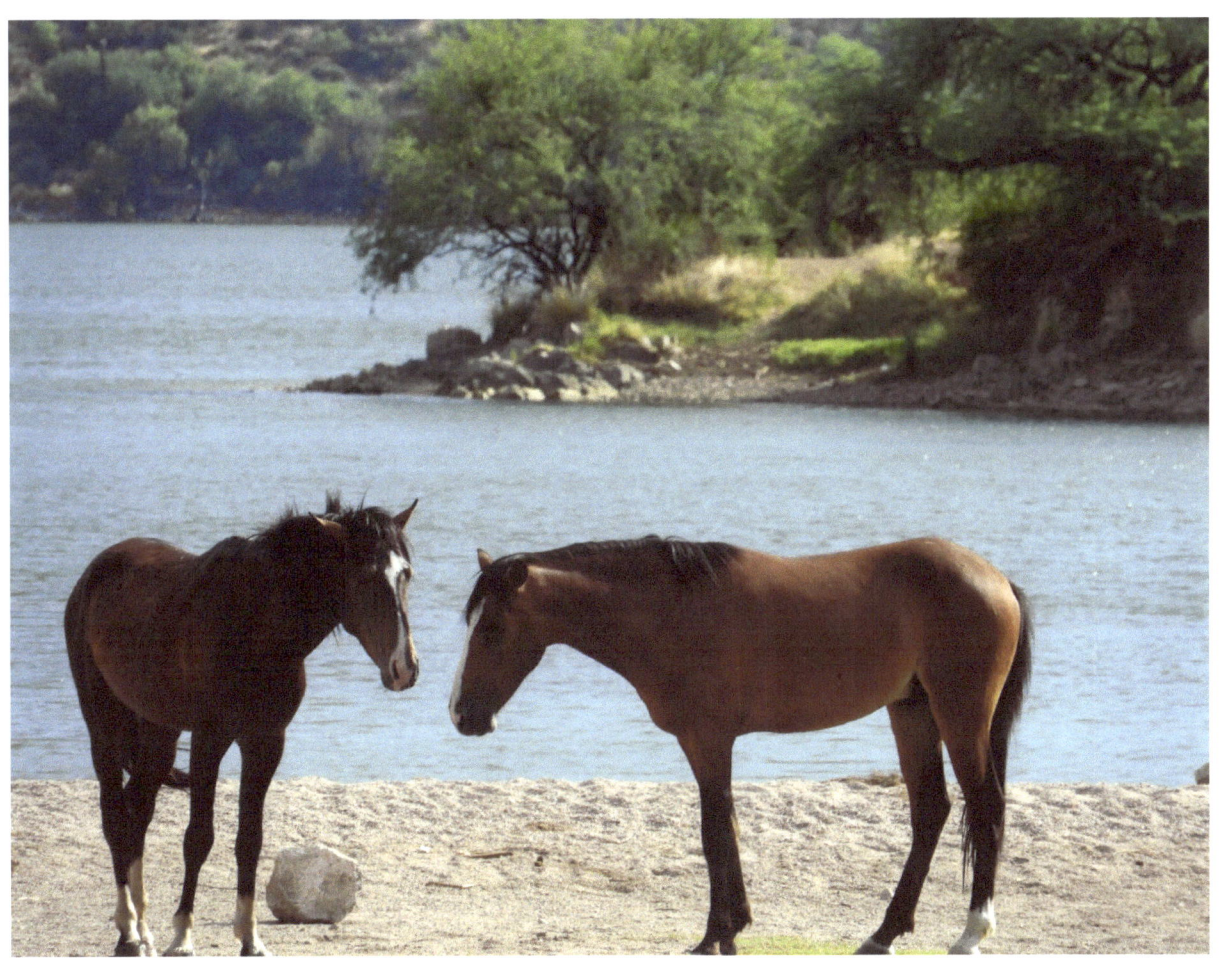

Despite this there are proposals that would allow the round-up and slaughter of wild horses.

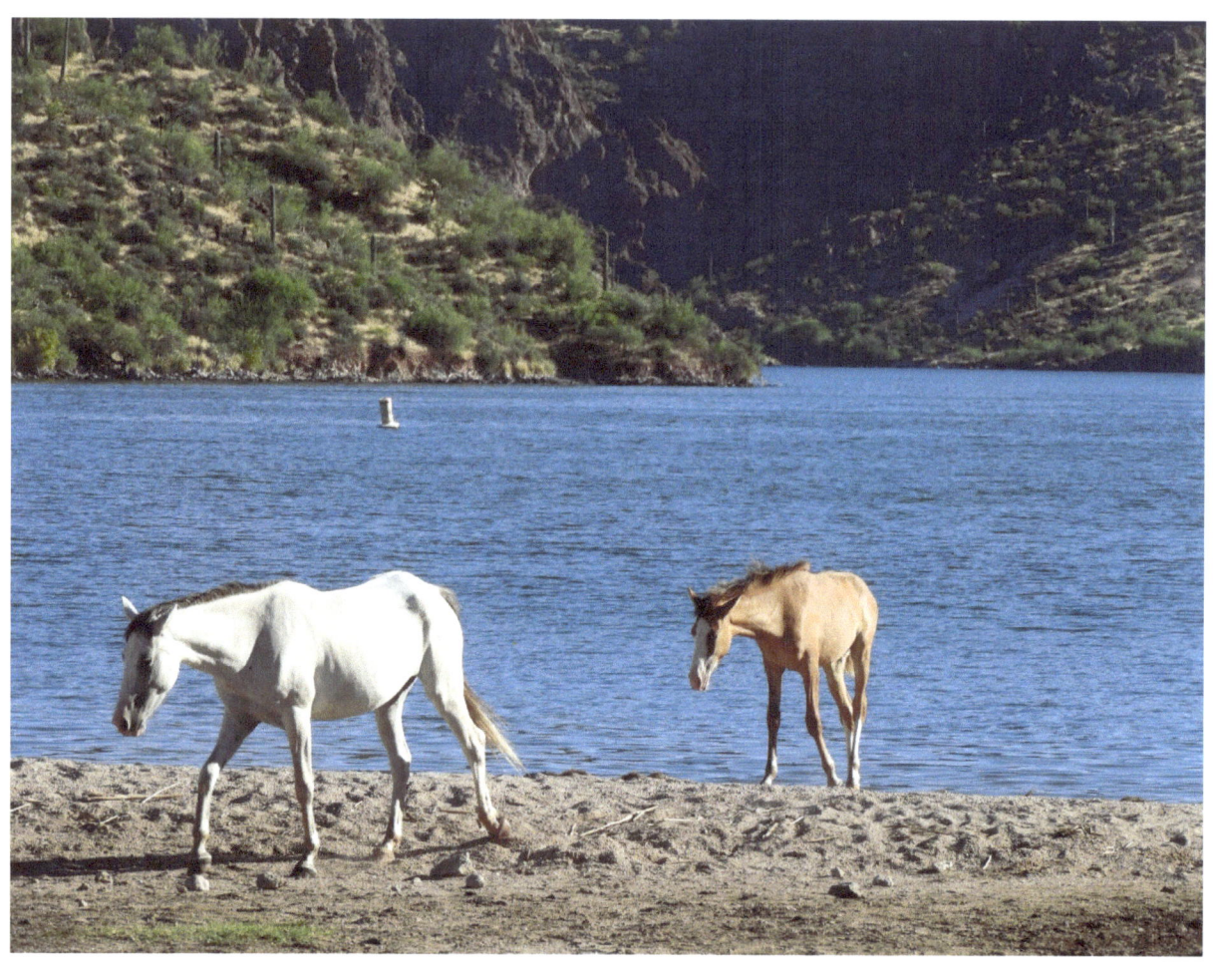

If that is allowed to happen, scenes like this one would not exist except in books and memoried.

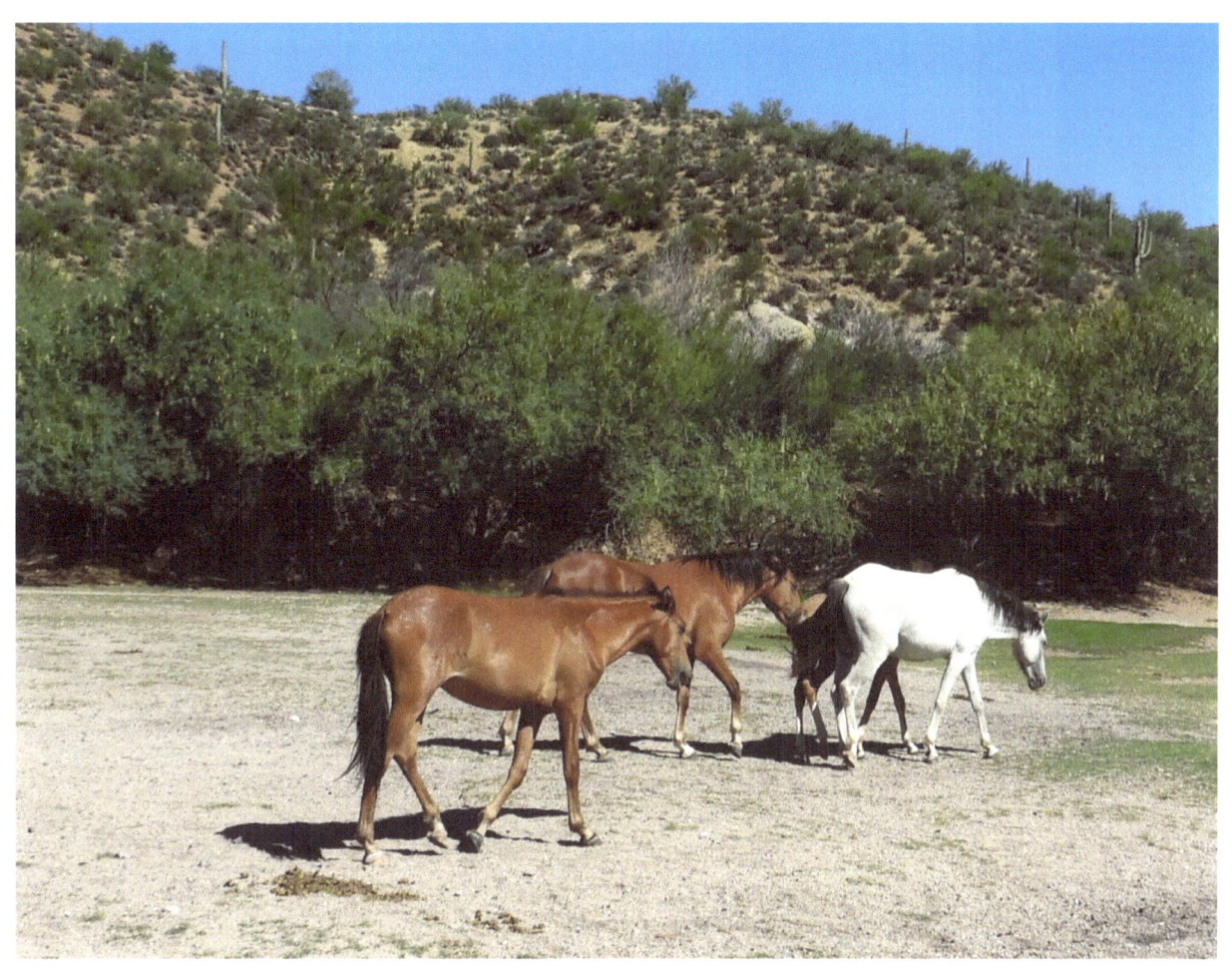

The wild horses of the United States deserve better.

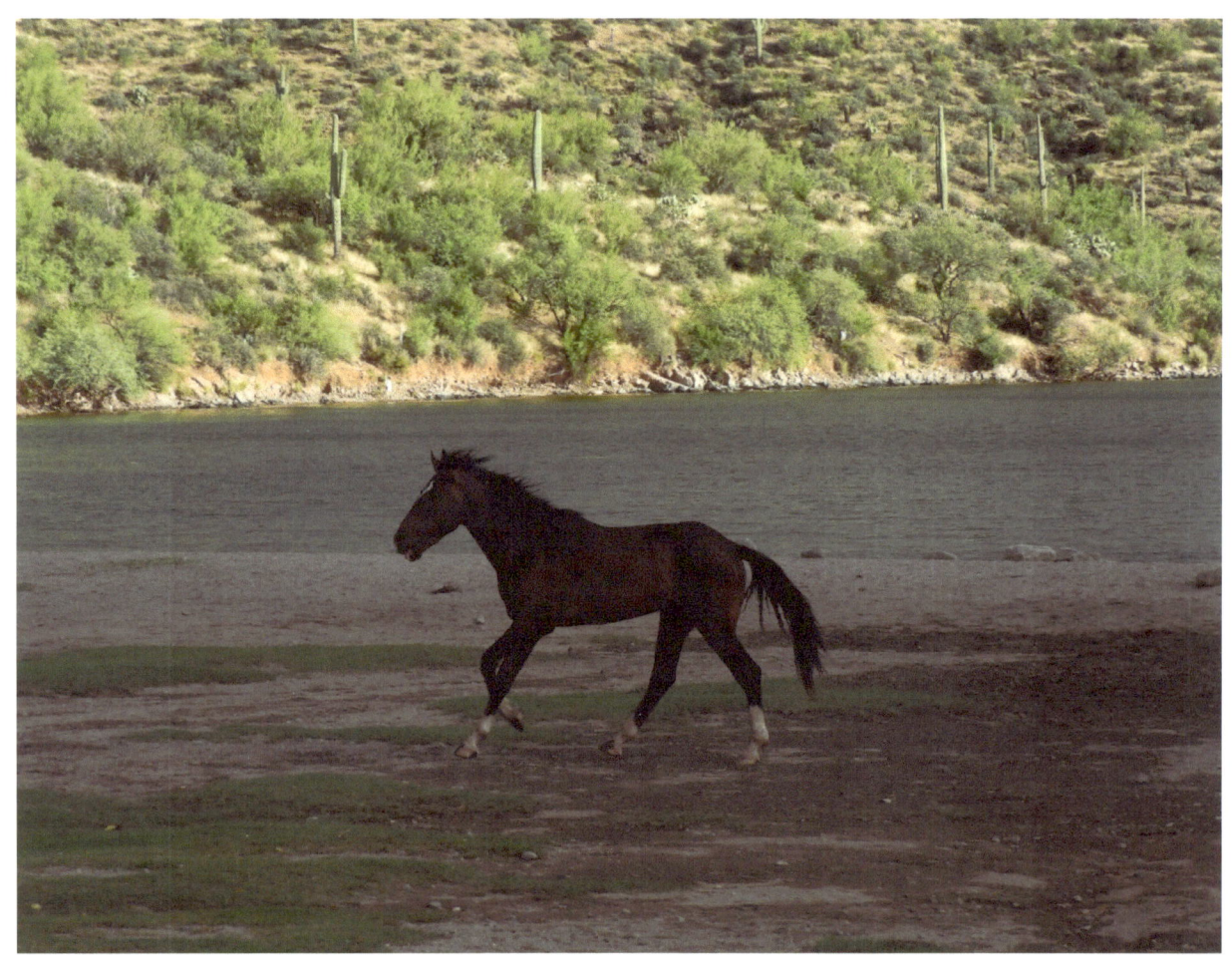

They deserve to be allowed to live free and wild as they have done for centuries.

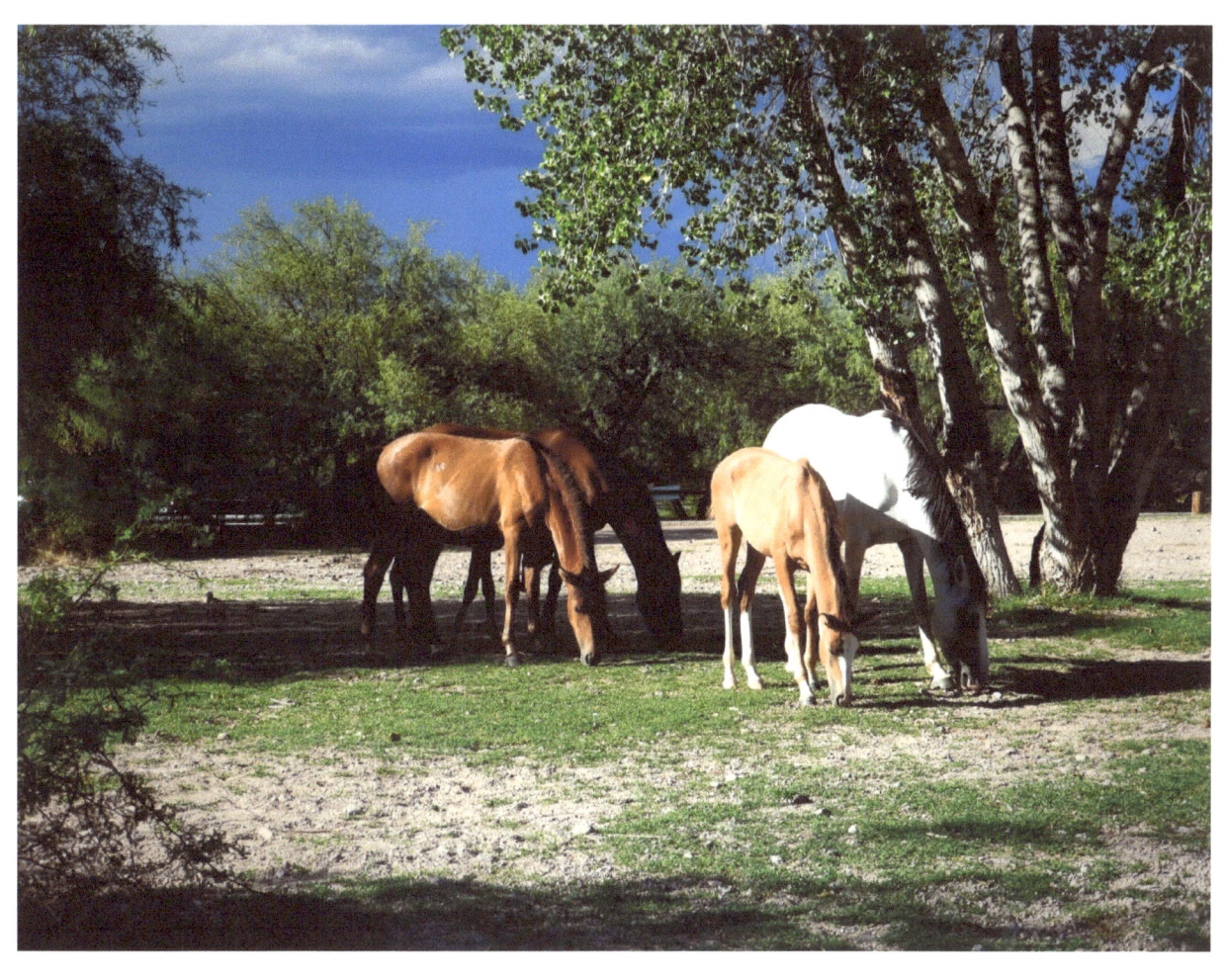

The wild horses need your support. DON'T LET THEM BECOME HISTORY!

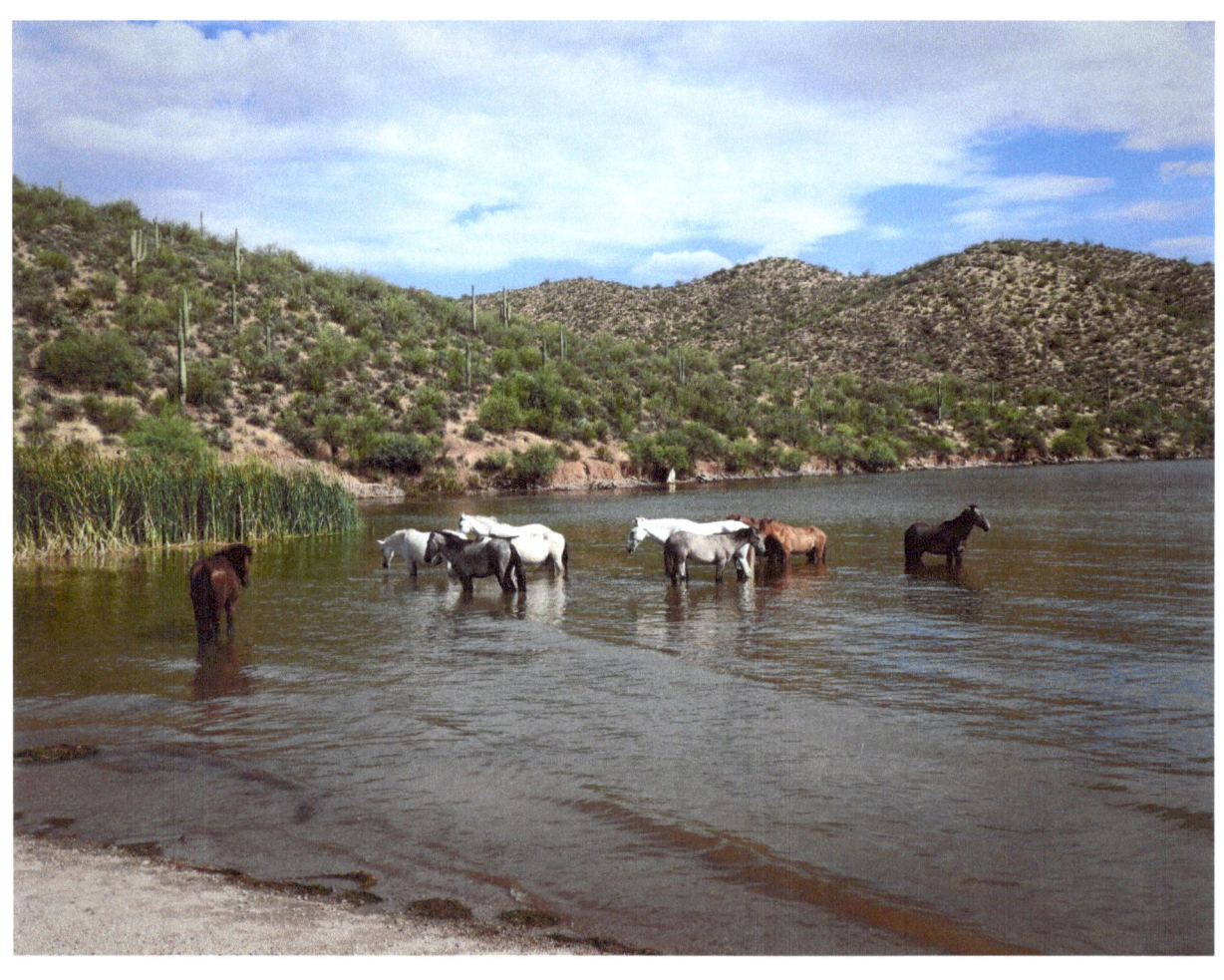

Keep them wild and free for our children and generations to come to enjoy.

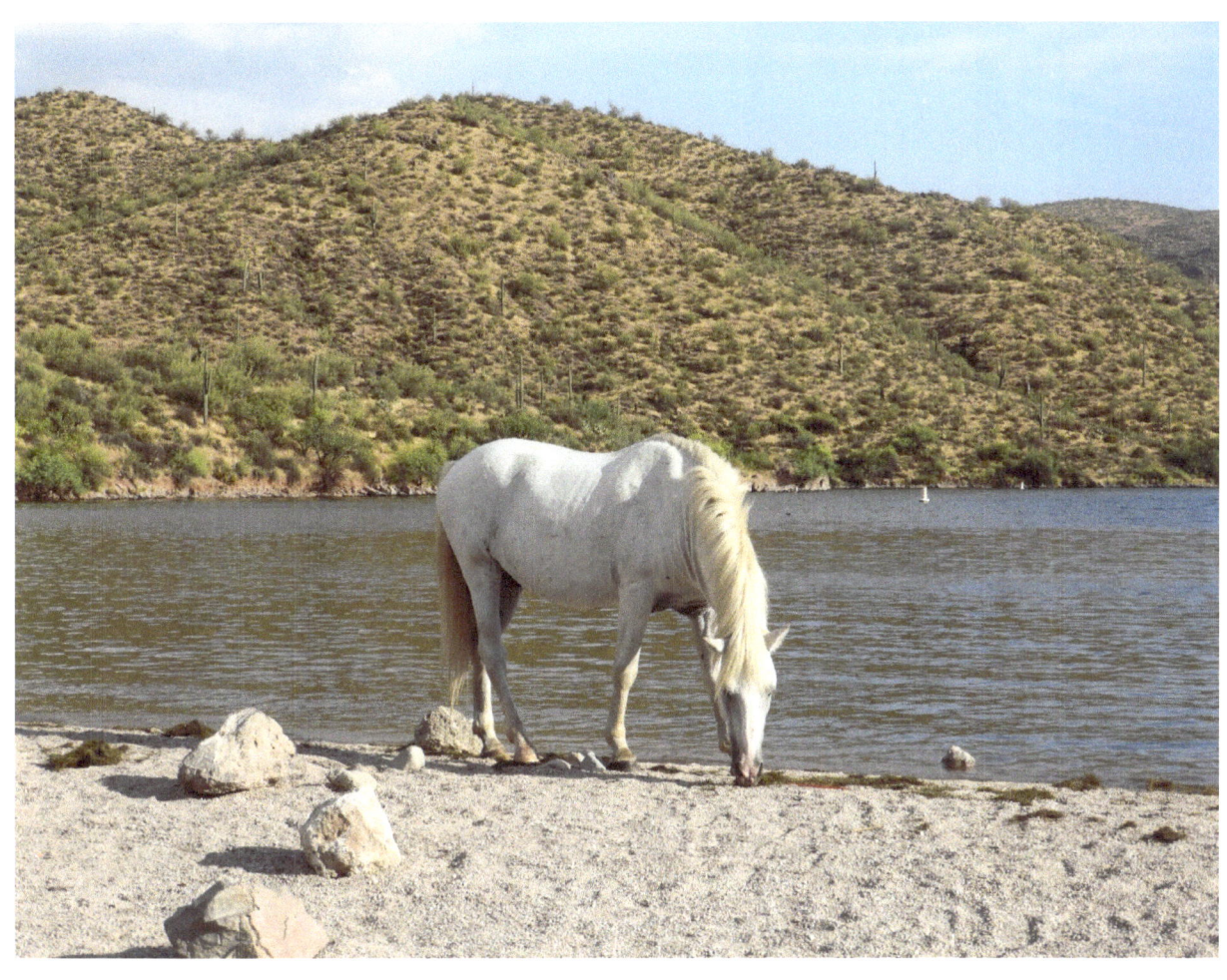

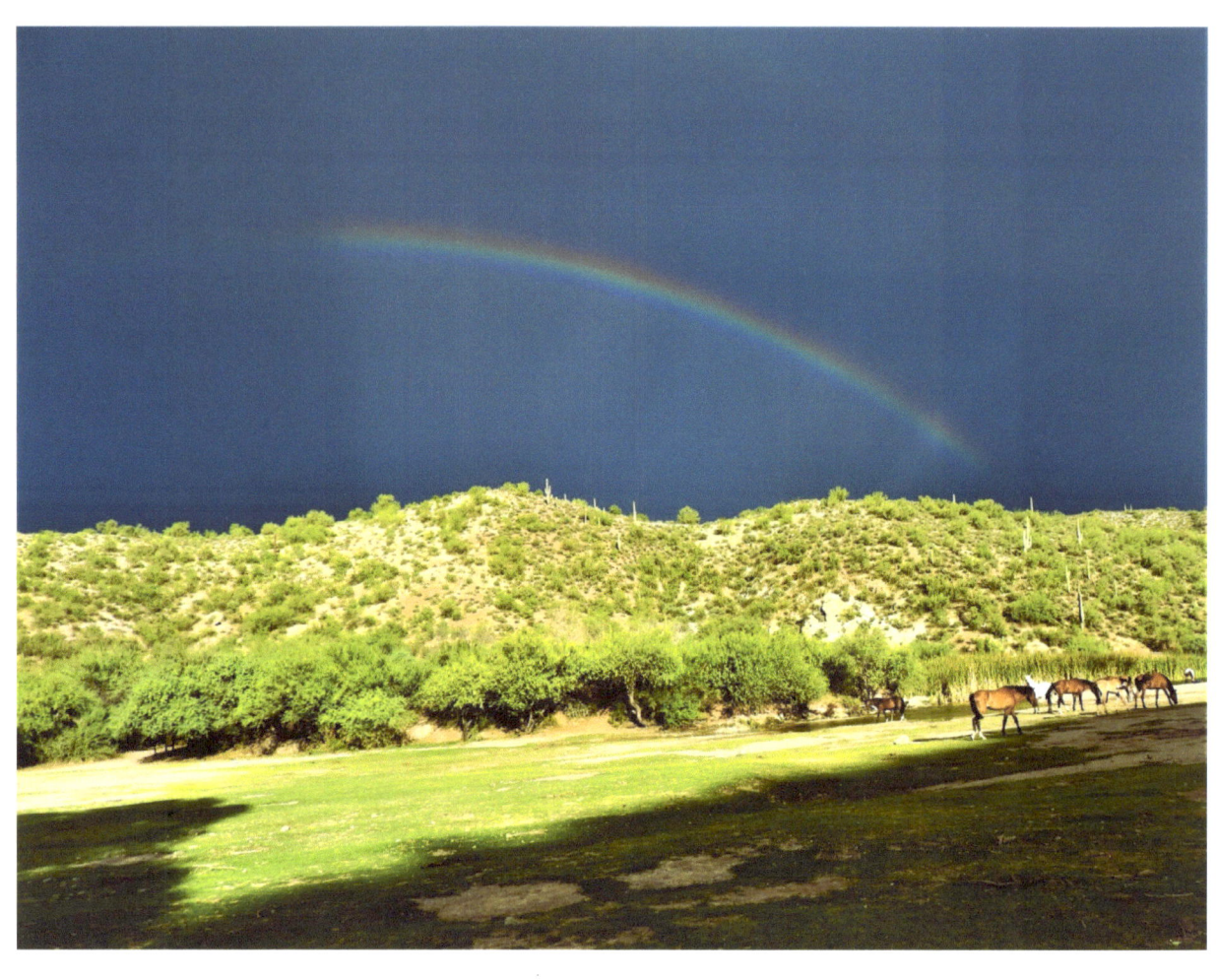

At the end of the Rainbow …

the pot of gold is a band of wild horses!

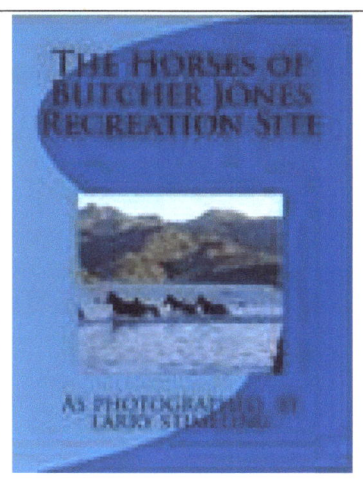

THE HORSES OF BUTCHER JONES RECREATION SITE

Photographs of the Salt River Wild Horses that frequently visited the Butcher Jones Recreation Site in the Tonto National Forest near Mesa, Arizona. A portion of the proceeds will be donated to the Salt River Wild Horse Management Group a 501(c)3 nonprofit organization dedicated to protecting the Salt River...

List Price: $30.00

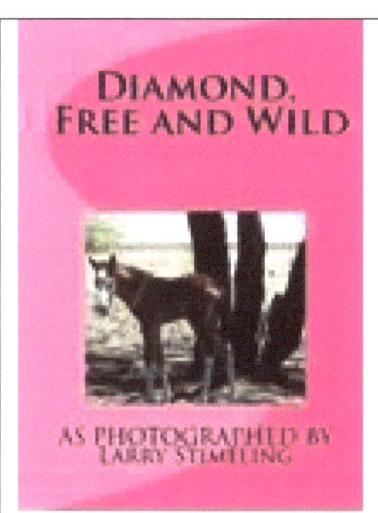

DIAMOND FREE AND WILD

Photo-biography of Diamond, one of the Salt River Wild Horses.

List Price: $20.00

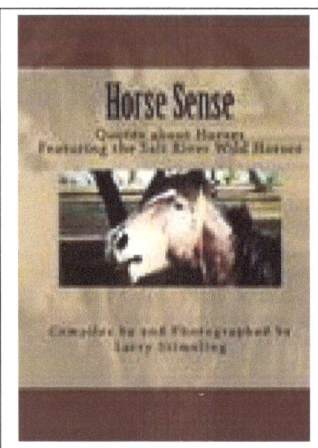

HORSE SENSE

A compilation of Quotes about horses especially wild horses. These sayings are paired photographs of the iconic wild horses ehat make the area along the lower Salt River near Mesa Arizona their home.

List Price: $15.

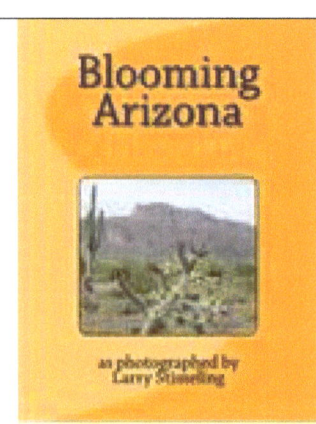

BLOOMING ARIZONA

Photographs of the beautiful flowers growing in Arizona.

List Price $20

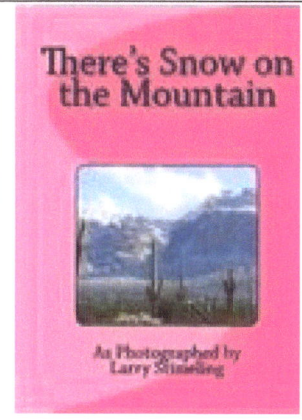

THERE'S SNOW ON THE MOUNTAIN

Larry Stimeling takes you to see the beauty of thedesert mountain when it is covered with snow.

List Price: $10.00

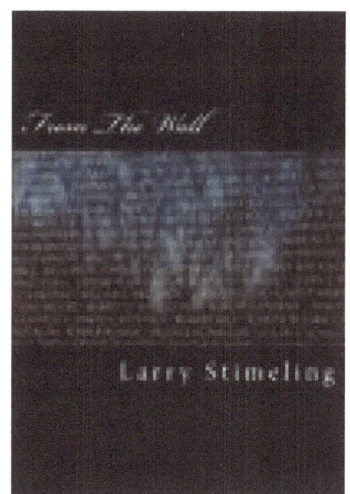

FROM THE WALL SECOND EDITION
A compilation of information and stories about some of the men and women whose names are on the Vietnam Veterans Memorial. The information was gathered from several data bases. The stories are personal accounts of incidents that happened during his visits to displays of the replicas of The Wall.
List Price: $20.00

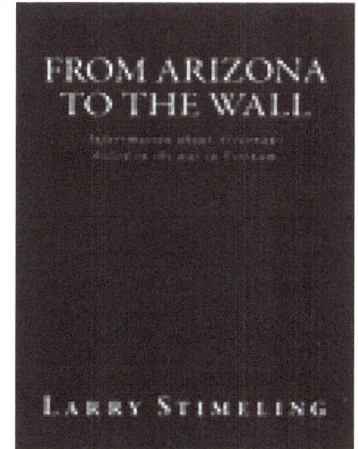

FROM ARIZONA TO THE WALL
A companion book to From The Wall, From Arizona to the Wall is a compilation of information about those who died in the Vietnam War, Those who never returned (MIAs) and those who died later

| | from Agent Orange exposure or PTSD related suicide. Included in the book are interesting facts about the Vietnam... List Price: $12.50 |

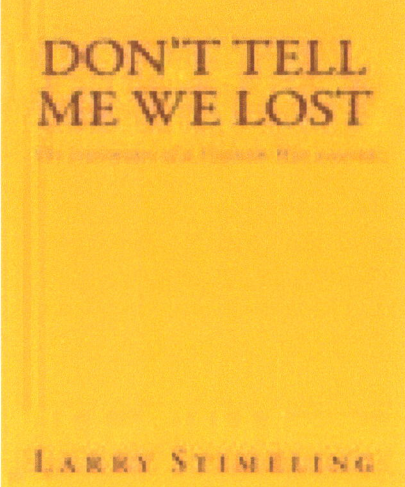

ON'T TELL ME WE LOST

A Vietnam Veteran's perspective on the perceived outcome of the war and the things that influenced that perceived outcome.

Publication Date: December 24, 2015

List Price: $10.00

www.ingramcontent.com/pod-product-compliance
Lightning Source LLC
Chambersburg PA
CBHW041935240526
45473CB00034B/1654